Preface

Life

1. Being & Doing
2. Loving and
3. Truth

Death

1. Belongs to
2. In the universe
3. My place
4. Go
5. It
6. Let
7. Start to
8. I won't actually die
9. Care to be aware
10. Too much outside on my inside
11. Faithfully forget it
12. Nostalgia and opportunity cost set expectations
13. The river flows from my biological source too
14. The light is always there
15. I'm not the only one
16. An infinite and finite obviously cloudy paradox
17. Of course I know how
18. Beauty is cliché
19. Zen isn't cliché
20. More more more more more! Next! Again!
21. Hell precedes heaven, death precedes birth, assuming they are real
22. Guns, sometimes sparkly obnoxious flamboyant psychological projections
23. Overthrow the errors of my brain
24. Self anarchy is the beginning
25. Stop editing myself
26. Grace and mercy in discomfort
27. Promises are labels too
28. I didn't get enough as a child, so what
29. People watch to know myself
30. Seeing me through them
31. Traits are unlearned too
32. There's cortisol in tears
33. More is tiring
34. Being is wisdom
35. Don't let my strength take my soul
36. Ego death brings me closer…
37. To my true self
38. Breath tames the brain

39. Dig for and denounce the labels
40. I'm always invited to the party in my heart
41. "I need, I need to do more, what's next?! I want it all, but I'm afraid of it!?"
42. "I just need to, umm? Just this one last time, then I'm done? I think?"
43. "I don't know, I mean, I just, I wish, I can't!"
44. "I'm special! Yippee! Us versus them!"
45. "I do it to win and not feel like a loser!!!"
46. "Alright, well, it was nice talking?"
47. Music is for my soul so turn off the podcast and shake that ass
48. Being ok with death brings bountiful life
49. Don't test others, embrace them
50. Distrusting my brain to lead it to peace
51. Denial of self brings freedom
52. Do I really need to belong?
53. Put the weights down, and stop running to the finish
54. Go somewhere new without it, and ask for directions back
55. Nurturing Doubt
56. Candy coated blue screens of depression that crush dreams
57. Yes, I can get satisfaction
58. Do the opposite
59. Ascent leaves little energy for descent
60. My brain made it a big deal, not me
61. Money is a way to share
62. Not trying can be petrifying
63. A misguided best can bring out the worst
64. It has no motive
65. Formalities are rigid, move
66. If I don't mean it, I smile quietly
67. The Kool-Aid is still laced with cyanide
68. Intestines are a metaphor for life
69. The natural choice is the hardest because we do not choose
70. Listening, watching, tasting, and feeling keep me from the smell of the roses
71. Control opposes balance
72. Walking as the crow flies is dangerous without wings
73. Be centered, not perfect
74. "How do I survive without a phone?!"
75. A new form of loneliness
76. The modern antithesis of it
77. The three headed monster
78. Right or wrong, anticipation leads to judgment
79. My true center is simple
80. Stop for satisfaction, keep searching for discontent
81. My love is not a language, language is limited, and love is unlimited

Preface

If you have the e-book, please have a notepad and pen by your side.

This book will teach you to swim. If you don't want to know about yourself, or you're afraid of what you'll dig up then you will really benefit from this. If you're happy always doing, being busy, and feeling that low level anxiety sprinkled with overwhelm all the time then this book might be the thing to rock you out of it.

The mind is a front, it's a put on. All of your answers in this book ALL of them are subjective. They're subjective to your past experiences, and your thoughts on the future. None of them MUST be true. They can help guide you through the veil of your mind to find your truth. The greats: Lao Tzu, Maharishi, Jesus Christ, Buddha, etc. all say the SAME thing, you must die to self. I must die?! What? Not literally... It's a figure of speech.

What is self? Self is a story you tell over and over for attention. Self is a phrase, word, mannerism, sound, posture, action, etc. you use that you heard or saw somewhere else. Self is any imitation of another, in life, from television or movies, from music. Self is the thing that looks for security or certainty. Self is the thing that looks to feel important by acting out, or keeping it in. Self is the thing that wants to hold on to emotions. Self is the thing that is afraid of failure and is drawn to pleasure when failure comes. Self is the thing that makes judgments and has preferences. Self is the source of all suffering. Even though we're groomed to fit in and to feel "belonging," our souls know the truth. We don't need to fit into anything, or belong to anything but life.

Have you ever "blacked out" without drinking alcohol? You're driving somewhere, and you don't remember getting there. You're having a conversation and you hear yourself saying AMAZING insightful things but you can't remember a thing you said and after think "what did I say, I wish I wrote that down, it was really good!" That's called your consciousness. That's when your mind steps out of the way and your truth is coming through. That's when the programming has stopped. That's when you don't have to recall something you said before to sound sure, right, or important. Nothing is certain, there is no right or wrong, and importance is trivial.

What if you didn't have a preference?

This is where your mind says "what does he mean? ... What if I didn't have a preference? Huh?

The point of this book is the blank space
This book is not about what I mean
This book is about perception
Deeper than critical thinking
Undoing critical thinking
So you're not so critical

Again... what if you didn't have a preference?

History is a distraction from the now
Pain is temporary and situational
Suffering is selfish

Life

1 – Being & Doing

What if we didn't have to do anything, to be anywhere, or to be anyone?

What if we had to do everything, to be everywhere, and be everyone?

What if we were leaves on the forest floor?

What would we do as leaves?

2 – Loving and

When is love?

Where is love?

What is love?

Who is love?

There is no who
There is no what
There is no where
There is no when
There is no why
How is to be
One with oneness
Truth in awareness
Shared and sharing it
Love and loving
I am your and I am it
It is and it is I
To be begin not being

3 – Truth

Nothing seems real
Life is an ironic paradox
We don't have fixed identities
Our personalities are not us anymore
Love blasts through every pore of our bodies
We've done the work, we have daily practices, and we feel it
No one and nothing can take this from us, we are rediscovered
The journey is complete and we're just along for the beautiful ride of life
Seeing can be belief so to clear our brains of things we've seen we use our voices
Sound is subtle so to clear our brains of things we've heard we use our voices
We share these things with our loved ones, all roads lead to love, even fear
Paper has no empathy, journaling pales in comparison to talking with us
The more our brains are aware of themselves the more we can clear
Share it all before it gets buried and becomes us
Peeling back our onion is easier this way
The way to living is truly connected
The way to living a conscious life
The way to truth
The way to love
The way to me
The way to us

When is our truth?

Where is our truth?

What is our truth?

Who is our truth?

Death

1 – Belongs to

Nature
Receive
Turn it off
I am sacred
Be in awe of myself
The eighth rung is me
Self care practiced then
Night and dusk are sacred
Morning and sunrise are sacred
Not about internal first impressions
I learn about external first impressions
Sifting through the chaos of the brain to find the gold of the heart is a daily practice
The brain has 100 billion complex neurons so then does complexity create fear?
The heart has 4 simple chambers so then does simplicity create love?
When my eyes are closed I have to be to open them
I don't know anything about 96% of the universe
Inner space is more accessible than outer space
Make space within the space and hold it
Oneness doesn't scratch the surface
No words to express the gratitude
Synchronicity is everywhere
No words in any language
Everything is everything
Life is a metamorphosis
Life is a coincidence
Life is an accident
Life is a chance
Be my life
I'll see

2 – In the universe

Motivated to trap me in fake billion dollar machines of smoke and mirrors, Silicon dreams
Dropped the e so they could drop technological e on me and trap me in their fake Molly
The war on drugs is still going, the new drug pushers are making billions hiding my soul
To be motivated by the universe and radiate soul and truth and see the synchronicity
To be motivated by survival based feelings of pain and pleasure and feel conflicted
To be motivated by intuition and know choice and power exist but feel like a loop
I can choose what I'm motivated by, but the ultimate choice is a difficult paradox
To see the forest through the trees I have to truthfully enter the forest
I lived in a loop perpetuated by the ideas of life, death, and money
I have the ability to slow the loop down and even stop it
My brain and conscious mind are forever on a seesaw
I have the ability to rebalance the seesaw of me
Animals aren't concerned with life or death
Once I realize nothing is what it seems
The need to know vanishes
Take my phone
Leave it home
Can I?   I'll know myself

Stop being quiet, use my voice
Separation anxiety is human
Put it down and speak up
I could use a break
It won't miss me
It feels nothing
It won't know
Brain hacking
The Valley
Dopamine
It will beg
Please
Come
Back

Living every day like it's my last leads to anxiety, illness, and fear because I don't want to die
Living each day like it's my first leads to wonder, and health because I wish to live
Conscious fear of loss and subconscious loneliness are invasive
Does social media make me feel less social and more alone?
I inevitably lose someone or something
Death is the only certainty of life
It's time I lost time
Lose the old me
Deny myself
See the real
The reality
The self
That

3 – My place

Meditation is a gift tailored for me, no one else is given my gift… how could they be?
A healthy practice will use meditation as a tool in the toolkit but know it's one tool
A healthy practice will incorporate both preventative and emergency work
Not knowing what will come, not controlling, and being open
Meditating in nature alone seems like a responsible way
Be careful how much I meditate and what I want
Be careful who I meditate with if I do it socially
Be careful with intentions, intentions of brain
My meditation will evolve as I evolve
Meditation is different for everyone
Meditation can be overwhelming
Meditation can be nervousness
Meditation can be depression
Meditation can be delusion
Meditation can be a label
Meditation can be active
Meditation can be dance
Meditation can be song
Meditation can be bliss
Be open to receiving
There is no right

There I am	Floating down my river of unknown
My gift	People think I'm crazy or drugged
To sit	I am everything right now
To be	I am myself right now
I	I am it

The eighth rung is the most inconceivably beautiful thing in the universe
The seventh rung is truth that naturally flows from my true soul
The sixth rung is forgiveness that's unexplainably liberating
The fifth rung is self destruction and it is a motherfucker
The fourth rung is self vulnerability which is scary
The third rung is respect of the awareness
The second rung is self awareness
The first rung is self care
Do not skip rungs
I could fall

It scared my heart because my brain was completely out of control
I woke up, took a shower and thought about killing him
I wanted to run him over in his own car
It changed my life, it was not me
Meditation saved my soul

Next time I'm in my car, somewhere I'm away from anyone that will think I'm insane
There are seven phrases to yell, scream at the top of my lungs, they're obvious
Affirmations and incantations are based in delusion, but they're a start
I AM NOT ANYONES BULLSHIT BELIEFS
I AM NOT ANYONES OPINION OF ME
I AM NOT ANYONES JUDGEMENTS
I AM NOT MY CHILDHOOD
I AM NOT MY MOTHER
I AM NOT MY FATHER
I AM NOT MY PAST
Journal about these
Talk about these

Where do I feel out of control in my life?

Unknow to come back to my source
Unknowing is beautifully vulnerable
Allow myself to be out of control
Practice is mental operation
Internal order is practice
These are the first steps
There is no anesthesia
Operate on my brain
The tools are in me
Nowhere to go
My eyes closed
Uniquely mine
Nothing to do
Keep writing
Self therapy
Sit with it

"I told you so" is one step away from mental revenge
Forgiving is like rocket science when I'm closed
Forgiving falls into place when I let it
I have to forgive others first

What's the worst thing I've ever done to someone else?

What's the worst thing that's ever been done to me?

What's the worst thing I've ever done to myself?

What would it take for me to forgive myself for hurting another?

What would it take for me to forgive them for hurting me?

What would it take for me to forgive me for hurting myself?

Worst is a judgment, it's a duality, there is also best, neither is the truth
Black and white do not lead to self discovery, it's in the touch of grey
Forgiveness isn't a miracle, its part of an evolved practice
The formula for forgiveness is different for everyone
Forgiveness cannot be defined by a human
True forgiveness comes by accident
This is the most freeing part
Be open

Be open to it for it to come
Free them to free myself
Free myself for bliss

6 - Let

Something heavy is there
How do I do it?
This negativity
This activity
Change
How?

I may call myself weak for not having removed this from my life
I may judge myself even more for it now

Who have I blamed most in my life?

Who blames me?

Who else do I blame?

Or was it me?

I wish for mercy
I wish for grace
Stop blaming
Brain blames

7 – Start to

What's the metaphor in my suffering?

What am I looking for there?

Belonging?

Self destruction is the next step of the ladder
What do I want to destroy in my brain?

To want to destroy a part of my identity is a strong message to my brain
This could be a painful ride and sometimes masks itself as depression
Maybe I've been judging myself for not changing it
How do I change once I'm aware of it?
How do I destroy it to find the truth?
This thing I crave to change
What have I been trying?

Trying times are synonymous with difficult times
Abandon them to abandon my false self
Trying is stress and can overwhelm
Why do I try so hard?
What did I believe?

Don't try to get it   Trying is difficult
Life is easy   Slip into it
It's there   Under

8 – I won't actually die

Who do I want to help the most?

Could there be something there I'm looking for in myself?

Who am I when I'm closed?

Am I self destructive?

What do I do when I'm in self destruct mode?

Disapprove my brain
To help my mind
Find my heart
Fail my brain
Help myself

Suffering leads to soothing
It's part of life
I suffer
I grow
It passes

9 – Care to be aware

I may have bought into this self love trend
I can't jump to the top of a ladder
There are rungs to climb a ladder
Self care is the first rung

Where could I use the most care in my life?

How do I show care?

Who do I respect the most?

Reverence comes from wisdom
Respect comes from approval
Reverence is from the heart
Respect is from the brain
The brain approves
The heart loves

10 – Too much outside on my inside

They're the ones selling me lies that I believe because I'm a seeker, I'm type a, I want more, better
Gurus are selling bullshit, and have believed their own and robbed thousands for their billions
McDonalds has harmed billions of people, but they don't hide it with double talk and bullshit
Sorry to them for making their unresolved problems my problems and profiting from me
Sorry to them for feeling weak and powerless and doing nothing about it but projecting
Sorry to them for making me a perfectionist even thought they'll deny it until they die
Sorry to their systems they perfectly engineered to make me feel like I'm not it
Sorry to them for thinking I'm their guinea pig to help fix their own issues
Sorry to them for making me think like I need more to be someone else
Sorry to them for making me feel like I'm not doing enough
Sorry to them for making me feel like I need to be better
Sorry to them from cheating me out of being myself
Sorry to me for not knowing awareness is an option
Sorry to them for manipulating my emotions
Sorry to them for manipulating my identity
Sorry to them for blindly robbing my soul
Sorry to them for not knowing their truth
Sorry to their deaf hidden agendas

I'm already helped	It does not work
Understand this	Open my eyes
Listen for truth	Faith is power
Belief is weak	Don't believe
Watch them	Be me
Listen	Truth
Hear	Lies

When do I lie?

Do I lie to stay congruent?

11 – Faithfully forget it

What do I have faith in?

Who do I have faith in?

How do I show faith?

What's home like?

Time is a result of the word rhythm, is a result of the word vibration, is a result of true wordless love
Love is the only word in any spoken language that has a universal immovable moveable definition
A wonderfully ironic question: when in our development do we become concerned with time?
Not exposed to time, would we be aware of time, or simply the transition from light to dark?
A wise man, told me that time exists, and I asked him how he could be so sure of this
He told me that our heart beats and it keeps time in rhythm, like other body parts
Rhythm comes from vibration so I asked, what is the source of vibration?
He replied, it is Anahat, and to research that and come back to him
I did research Anahata, which is our heart chakra or center
The heart is the most pure organ in the body

Time is a perversion of rhythm to control   Faith is natural if I'm at home with myself
Rhythm and music are true   Celebrate, commemorate, and be myself
Deny time to find truth   Nostalgia is belonging to the outside
Truth is not a concept   Have faith in myself first
Time is not money   Nostalgia is dangerous
Raise my truth   True home is safe
Home is truth

12 – Nostalgia and opportunity cost set expectations

What talk didn't my parents have with me that I expected?
Birds and the bees?
Money?

I expected my parents to have had these talks with me, now think who their parents were
Knowing my grandparents is it fair of me to expect this of my parents?
Expectation is one of the biggest sources of human suffering
Who expects things? Children, dogs, and delusional people
Stop expecting my parents to have not done things to me
Stop expecting my parents to have done things for me
Stop expecting people to make responsible decisions
Stop expecting things from my government
Stop expecting black and white outcomes
Stop needing to see that justice is served
Expectation and entitlement are one
Stop expecting things from myself
Expectation is external
Entitlement is internal
You're an adult
Entitle myself
Stop labeling
Help myself
Grow up

What makes me nostalgic?

13 – The river flows from my biological source too

Who are/were my parents?

What did my parents do for me?

What did my parents do to me?

What were my parent's hobbies?

Would that make a rewarding career?

Accept them for both because I wouldn't be here without them
Don't condemn those that helped bring my soul here
Don't try to fix those that helped bring my soul here
Don't disown those that helped bring my soul here
Don't judge those that helped bring my soul here
Do I have the vulnerability to see?
It happened for a reason
It happened for me
Appreciate life

14 – The light is always there

There's a reason people say I can be selfish   Stop the loop
My brain is selfish, scared of sharing itself   Slow down
My brain is a loop of selfishness   How?

What are some beautiful things people have done for me?

They sensed that I was open
Open myself to receiving
Open myself in private
Open myself in public
Open my mind
Crack it
Free it

15 – I'm not the only one

What are some of my recurring thoughts I wish would disappear?

Where did they come from?

What's worse… a break, a burn, an ache, or death?
The brain is excellent at labeling
The heart doesn't label

Heartache	Let's give me a headache	
Heartbreak	Let's break my brain	Everyone dies, die to my false self
Heartburn	Let's burn my brain	This will free my true self
My soul is under it		My passionate soul

16 – An infinite and finite obviously cloudy paradox

Some entertainers are not really themselves
Kanye West is himself, I think

Who am I?

Am I?

Fit into myself by being different
Identity can be tied to anything
Don't hang my soul from it
The most painful death is   Suffocation of the soul
Appreciate myself   Be divergent to live
Stop conforming   Everyone does
Be different   Everyone is
Everyone is   Right?

17 – Of course I know how

Whatever I answered is real and no one can take from me
My body will decompose, but not my soul

Do I know someone who's taken their own life?

There's a wall between my subconscious self and my conscious self until I tap into it
Some build a wall between their public and private selves to protect something
If who I am in public isn't who I am in private
There's going to be a disconnect and issues
Being exposed could dissolve my brain
Being exposed could break my heart
Talk about it because we will listen
Expose myself, be vulnerable to it
Please be congruent for my soul
Rest in peace, you were gifts
The heart can never break
The soul is never gone
Chester Bennington   Let's break the barrier to integrate my subconscious
Chris Cornell   Let's break the barrier to raise my heart and soul
Please   Freedom from walls is bliss
Talk   Break down my walls

Public
―――――――――――――――――――――――――――――――――――――
Private
―――――――――――――――――――――――――――――――――――――
Subconscious
Heart
Soul

What if this was all one piece?

18 – Beauty is cliché

Fashion is a fad is a fantasy is a delusion is deception, am I lying to myself?
People did nothing to earn their bone structure, cartilage shape, and skin
The more full of myself I am, the less of myself I am
Be careful with what I perceive as beauty
The concept of beauty will disappear

How am I beautiful?

Who is beautiful?

What? is a peculiar question, it's a necessary question
What? typically spurs action, sometimes of the heart
The heart asks How? more than the brain does
The brain asks Why? more than the heart does
Where do I go? I need to be there soon!
FOMO oh no?! When is it happening?
The brain starts by asking what is it?
Who what where when why how?   Where do I love them?
What are my main questions?   When do I love them?
The hearts truth asks who?   Why do I love them?
Think about this each day   Conditionally
Question myself daily   Love is not

19 – Zen isn't cliché

What am I hiding?

What do I wear on my sleeve?

What would make my life simpler?

Deceit and dishonesty are not simple
Simplicity can answer a lot for us
Use my voice
Be honest
Be direct
Be fair

20 – More more more more more! Next! Again!

What's something I did yesterday that I want to fall away and not be a part of me?

What do I regret?

Do I have 20 workout routines? Do I work several jobs? Do I have multiple relationships? Do I put my money everywhere and invest and diversify?   Do I need to constantly rearrange things? Do I constantly clean because things are out of order? Do I let things get so messy because the thought of cleaning is too much? Do I feel like it's too much?

Where is there the most complexity in my life?

Do I regret what's complicated?

What does this relate to?

Complication doesn't make me better
I can have a sophisticated easy life
Complication clouds things
Ease clears them up
It clears me up

21 – Hell precedes heaven, death precedes birth, assuming they are real

Where did I come from? Who helped make me?

No one is self made, we came from somewhere
Needing to know is pain
Not knowing is bliss

What is the most painful thing in my life?

Is there a lack of trust there?

Remember falling as a child?
I trusted myself
It's ok to fall

What's my highest fall from grace?

Have I ever had a falling out with anyone?

Have I ever had a falling out with myself?

I get back up
To go down
The center

22 – Guns, sometimes sparkly obnoxious flamboyant psychological projections

Imagine my identities as different jackets
I can slip them on and off at will

Am I afraid of being too manly?

Am I afraid of being too feminine?

Do I want to be self made?

For some, being self made is a self granted douche permit
I did this, me, I made this, I slaved and worked
Men, it's not sexy or cool to be a douche
The media made that sexy and cool
Father time is ticked and tockless
Age has little to do with maturity
True cool and sexy is maturity
I had help to mature
Mother earth loves
Sexism isn't sexy
I make me

23 – Overthrow the errors of my brain

What makes me feel like a queen or king?
Dare I say a god?

When am I supremely confident?

Confidence is derived from the external world, brain, possessions, net worth, goals, etcetera
Humility is now associated with meekness, modesty, and passivity, but not confidence
Maybe confidence isn't such a good thing because it's the opposite of being humble
A lot of words like confidence in the Western English language could be updated
Confidence is derived from knowledge of the outer world and not the inner
Essence is derived from knowledge of the inner world and not the outer
External knowledge and accomplishment are peasants
Internal knowledge and failure are queen and king
Internal knowledge and failure bring ample gifts
Internal knowledge brings you true peace
Internal failure brings internal infinite
Essence is internal and forever
Humility is loved in failure
My brain needs to know
Failure of the known
Bankrupt my brain
God, I hate failing
God herself failed
Failing is painful
Failure is scary
Extra credit
Ego death
Be myself
Funeral
F+

24 – Self anarchy is the beginning

Do I remember my old self after making a choice that changed me?

Each day contains choice
Choice is not control

What is control?

What do I do to control?

Do I like being managed?

Freedom comes from chaos
Control is management
Don't control myself
Don't control others
Don't manage it
Surrender it
Forget it
Yield

Grace in conversation is not thinking of what to say next
Grace in conversation is not getting the last word
Grace in conversation is holding space
And not speaking to be heard

Have a real conversation	Be human
Don't over think	Be messy
Don't anticipate	Be now
Don't change it	Be real
Don't edit it	Be me

Do I feel graceful in conversation?

When am I courteous?

What's the last meaningful choice I made?

It's nice to be powerless
It's nice to have choice
Does free will exist?
Who chooses?
The universe?
Me?

26 – Grace and mercy in discomfort

When flies are buzzing around me, I let them
They will eventually land on my lips
I let them be

Why do I kill flies?

Is that true?

How big is my brain compared to a flies?

Am I sorry for killing living creatures?

Do I know a person that isn't graceful?

What do they do?

Have mercy
Be graceful

27 – Promises are labels too

The brain can commit a slow strangulation of the true self
Know myself to resuscitate myself, and feel my heartbeat
My brain suffocates my soul when I'm not aware of it

Where do I feel suffocated?

When did I last promise something?

When did I last mean it?

What can I promise myself that will keep me curious forever?

28 – I didn't get enough as a child, so what

They might be more comfortable being themselves than I am
The minute I stop trying to catch it is when I do
There's nothing to save, fix, help or do
Finally, I let myself slip away
I have the strength
Put it down

When do I need attention?

What do I wear to get attention?

What do I do to get attention?

Do I give enough attention to myself?

When is the last time I felt nurtured?

I don't need addictions anymore   They want things
I don't need attention anymore   I am at peace
Addict myself to myself   I am myself

29 – People watch to know myself

Where wants become needs that is where the shadow feeds

Who do I make fun of?

What do I say?

What could they possibly have that I want!?

Do I really want it?

A cold splash of water on the face reminds me of where I came from and what I am
This is hard work, this is where meditation and awareness practices shine
Sometimes I don't know how to watch how I watch others
This is a way to watch myself because it's a mirror
Seeing myself is the way into being myself
The reflections in the water help me
Help myself to unfog my mirror
See my reflections

30 – Seeing me through them

If I think someone is better than me, what do they have that I want?

If I think I'm better than someone, what do they have that I want?

Who has something I want?

Do I bully them in my head?

Don't be a dick
Be moderate
Be humane
Be tolerant

31 – Traits are unlearned too

Social Media is where I get to post about **exactly** who I am, right?

What's my personality like?

How much of my personality are traits I want?

Be careful not to latch on to a trait
Our personalities evolve

32 – There's cortisol in tears

I'm weak for crying
I label myself
I'm "strong"
I'm "afraid"

What am I labeled?

What makes me cry?

What could I cry about if I let myself?

Often there are tears under laughter
Once I cry the laughter is true
Not to be seen or to be heard
When it tickles my soul
When it's truly funny

33 – More is tiring

Pain is part of the past
The bliss comes later
Awareness is now

What else is there?

There's finishing to complete
There's always more
I'm complete
I've been

34 – Being is wisdom

Home is the most comfortable place there is
Heroin addicts say using is like going home
Home is where I can be myself
Not having to be anywhere
Not having to do anything
Not having to be anyone
Being me

How do I just 'be'?

Warm my heart
Open my mind
Clear my brain
Life

35 – Don't let my strength take my soul

This is where some of my self judgment comes from

When did I last say you're welcome?

What am I most aware of?

What am I most unaware of?

What am I most aware of about myself?

What am I most unaware of about myself?

What takes my awareness away?

What takes my openness away?

A closed mind knows everything
A cold heart comes from this
Love my power to receive
My vulnerability
My awareness
My openness
My love

36 – Ego death brings me closer…

People hate getting parking tickets more than they hate going to jail
Financial loss is scary, you won't have… money

Is death scarier though?

What do I want people to say about me at my eulogy?

Please answer it, go with the first sentence or few words, my gut

What do I want my most loved ones to say about me at my funeral?

The first gut reaction… "she was _____" "he was _____"
Nice, kind caring, smart, loving, a good person are typical simple responses
Close your eyes, the first thing is…?

37 – To my true self

Why do I feel like I'm not that?
Wait… what?

Why do I feel like I'm not those things I want loved ones to say about me at my funeral?
Pause, step back, this is how the work works, seeing myself under my brain
Now, what makes me feel like I'm not those things?
What past behaviors?

What I want loved ones to say about me at my funeral is mostly what I feel I'm not
This is a big part of my process and practice, stepping into my shadow
Explore this, now I'm seeing myself in order to free myself
Remember, the question why rarely creates a definite
Are those my true thoughts?

Where did they come from?	Theirs from the past
They might be from trauma	The pain is worth it
They might be delusion	As I shed my skin
The answer will change	Dying to live

38 - Breath tames the brain

Where do I feel like it's me against the world?

What gives me anxiety?

What overwhelms me?

What stresses me out?

Is it actually scary?

What's the worst?

Not knowing?

Guided breath can give me heavenly psychedelic experiences
Guided breath can dissolve the brain and slow the mind
I won't suffocate if I don't know what's next
Knowing isn't a human need
Security isn't a human need
I promise it isn't
Fog the mirror
Breathe deep
Exhale
Tingle
Hold

39 – Dig for and denounce the labels

What's out of order inside me?

Addiction is internal and external ignorance, excitement, dullness, strength, and weakness
Habit is external strength "I'm a type A achiever corporate athlete that wins" aka addict
Compulsion is internal weakness "I overeat and binge watch Netflix" aka addict
Ritual is external excitement "I go to yoga every M Tu Th at 7am" aka addict
Routine is internal dullness "I'm a homebody always cleaning" aka addict
Procrastination is external ignorance "I'm never finished" aka addict
Practice is internal order "Not attached, not doing" a free soul
Once I label myself an addict it creates an expectation
Don't let anyone stamp me or tag me with a label
I'm not a product on a shelf, I reject my label
Stop expecting myself to be an addict
Entitle myself to change the label
Entitle myself to know yourself
Stop and listen to your voice
Find my internal wisdom
Find my internal power

Things beyond memory	The roots of this could be in my childhood
Deep below traumas	Even deeper back to my ancestors
Deeper than I know	Through my grandparents
Below myself	Through my parents
Below reality	Rid myself of this
But above	It was them
Lie down	It's not me
Guided	Slowly
Alone	Find it
Being	Peace

40 – I'm always invited to the party in my heart

What's the worst thing I do to myself, and judge myself for after each instance?

What's my worst habit, ritual, procrastination, compulsion, routine, addiction?

What makes me feel out of alignment that I do to myself or let happen to me?

What breaks me?

What if today was the last day it ever happened?

How would I celebrate?
What do I imagine?
What would I do?

Good, now go do it
Put the book down
I mean it
GO

41 – "I need, I need to do more, what's next?! I want it all, but I'm afraid of it!?"

What are my addictions?

What were my old addictions?

A particular substance, thing, or activity
It's time to update the dictionary
I don't have any addictions?
Sure I do, label them
Labels are not truth
The system labeled
See that truth
See myself
Defined
By me

42 – "I just need to, umm? Just this one last time, then I'm done? I think?"

What are my compulsions?

What were my old compulsions?

Compulsion is the act of compelling; constraint; coercion and also an unhealthy obsession
Sales people are compelling, prisoners are constrained, and coercion is intimidating
Stop being sold, break free, be calm, and be healthily obsessed with myself
Compulsion is internal weakness
There isn't any more

43 – "I don't know, I mean, I just, I wish, I can't!"

What are my procrastinations?

What were my old procrastinations?

Procrastination is putting off or delaying, especially something requiring immediate attention
Procrastination is something I judge myself for, the fear of the unknown
Give myself immediate attention, learn it and do it, or don't
Procrastination is external ignorance
There's nothing to be afraid of

44 - "I'm special! Yippee! Us versus them!"

What are my rituals?

What were my old rituals?

Ritual is an established or prescribed procedure for a religious or other rite to belong
Rituals are a way to belong, but what if belonging to life itself satisfied that urge?
Find the belonging in myself, it never left
Ritual is external excitement
I can stop looking

45 – "I do it to win and not feel like a loser!!!"

What are my habits now?

What were my old habits?

Habit is an acquired behavior pattern regularly followed until it has become almost involuntary
Habits are powerful or weak, habit creates duality, black or white, but there are middles
Let myself go, be involuntary, don't think, and be spontaneous because life is
Habit is external strength
I already won

46 – "Alright, well, it was nice talking?"

What are my routines now?

What were my old routines?

Routine is a customary or regular course of procedure, normal ordinary and unremarkable
Routine is a way to hide and feel numb, hide from and numb what? It's there, in me
Give myself a procedure and turn it off, it's painless, I'm remarkable
Routine is internal dullness
I can have fun

What would I do if this was my first day on earth?

Guesstimated, I spend 29 seconds a day fearing death, and 9,000 seconds fearing time and money
Nothing related to time or money is ever inevitable, so then why do I spend my thoughts there?
What else would my brain think about if it were at peace with the inevitable? Being present?!
We dream about death so often and when we're awake we barely think about it, strange
Fear of not having enough money is death of status and security, but they're useless
Fear of what others will think of me is death of belonging, but I belong already
Fear of being unhealthy is death of the physical body, but that's inevitable
Fear of not being enough is death of the brain, but the heart is enough
Fear of loss of it is death of a part of you, but we are oneness
Our current consciousness tricks us into these wasteful ideas
Fear of not having enough money or time is fear of death
The word enough is mostly tied to time and money, odd
Will I have enough time? Will I have enough money?
The word enough tied to identity will bring insanity
My soul doesn't give a flying fuck about enough
Money reminds me of time with pressure
Money and time are inventions
Death of the body will happen
Stop trying and predicting
Too much energy wasted
My soul needs energy
Energy is the start
Start ascending
Stop wasting
And grow

48 – Being ok with death brings bountiful life

What would I die for?

Am I peaceful?

Being ready to die is a pure independence
Death of the brain leads to rebirth
There is freedom in death
Freedom from money
Freedom from time
Death of a belief   July 4th is the only US holiday with an alias of the date and nothing more
Death of an idea   4th of July is an excuse for some to pass time and get drunk
Death of a trait   Do I feel my Independence when I'm bound by time?
Declare peace   Is getting drunk a fear of living, or a fear of death?

Let's go to happy hour after being unhappy
Fear of wasting time so I get "wasted"
Further repressing my emotions
Beer tears come from delusions
Make drinking great again
Wait, it was never great
True independence
Make my life great

49 – Don't test others, embrace them

I'm expected to be the problem solver
I'm expected to "know" the future
I can falter knowing
Leave the knowing
Leave the test
"I know"
Toxic

Would I keep talking to someone who knew everything I was saying?

Put myself in their shoes

What is empathy?

Who's someone that hasn't heard from me in a while?

Don't reach out because I want something
Reach out because they want it

50 – Distrust your brain to lead it to peace

What don't I trust?

Who don't I trust?

What do I want to lead?

I see untrustworthy people in my screen	Confidence is trust of the outside world
Do not follow them	Do not care more about it than myself
Do not trust them	Caring too much leads to worry
Trust myself	I learn to worry from worriers
Lead myself	I learn to lead from love

51 – Denial of self brings freedom

We're taught to have self confidence for our brains but our heart doesn't know what that is

What am I not?

I am not…

I am not…

What am I right now that I don't want to be anymore?

I am not…

I am not…

I try too hard to be something
Try being nothing
The source
You

52 – Do we really need to belong?

Where do I not fit in?

What do I like to talk about?

What causes or issues make me want to speak up?

Where do you feel like I can't speak up?

What do I doubt about myself?

Occam's razor is the easiest sales tactic to sell people who doubt themselves
False prophets will try to sell me, cajole me, and control me
Don't respect anyone more than I respect myself
Beware of gurus that say they aren't
Beware of reverse psychology
Respect everyone equally
Doubt my own doubts
Doubt them
Doubt me

53 – Put the weights down, and stop running to the finish

The progression of human judgment ends in asking why
Judgment is a mirror showing you your brain
I am not my emotions or thoughts
My heart is beyond the mirror
Its opposite is judgment

Am I aware of it?

Think of something I do to make myself vulnerable
How am I socially vulnerable?

Vulnerability for vulnerabilities sake simply feeds the brain
Vulnerability in letting go will awaken me
The easiest path is relinquishment
I don't need protection

54 – Go somewhere new without it, and ask for directions back

How could I have been so stupid?
How could I have been so blind?
I told myself I wouldn't do this
Did I take my own happiness?
I can't believe I did it again
What did I do to lose this?
Why can't I stop this?
This always happens
Why is it this way?
Why did I do this?
That wasn't smart
Was it me?
Again…

What do I want to stop doing to myself?

I might go looking for the happiness
I might go on a judgment safari
Where did my happiness go?
Who took my happiness?
Who took it from me?

OMG where did it go?
"Look at this…"
"Unbelievable!"
"What a dick"
Remember?

Do I need happiness?
Am I sure?

Do I need to be fulfilled?
Am I sure?

Fulfillment is for warehouses
Fulfillment is completion
I'm already complete
Remember

56 – Candy coated blue screens of depression that crush dreams

What happens to me when I'm not happy?

What do I do to others when I'm not happy?

What do I do to myself when I'm not happy?

Blue screens and sugar are the new narcotics
Putting me to sleep, controlling me
Making me numb to life's joy
Wake up, put it down
Outcomes suck
I lose winning
I'm a spitter
Swallow life
Can't I see?
Spit it out
To live

57 – Yes, you can get satisfaction

Have I ever had that feeling I know is exactly what I want?
Things click and I'm connecting with people effortlessly
I feel clarity, calm, cool, and confident

What's that feeling for me?

What's the feeling I want?

Everything falling into place
Effortlessly you
In the zone
Samadhi
Wu wei
Flow

58 – Do the opposite

What's my bottom?

Wearing the shirt at the gym so they know I completed the race
Lifting the shaky uncomfortable amount so they see
Knowing what music is cool so I can be
Being able to drink enough
Running so many miles
Having a net worth
Getting the medal
Owning property
Having more sex
Passing the test   Where there's a top, there's also a bottom
Buying a ring   My top is my bottom
The top   It's one

59 – Ascent leaves little energy for descent

What's the top for me?

What are my goals?

A friend with a nine figure company questioned me if he was fulfilled
He was walking up the mountain and enjoying the walk to the top
I was trying to run up the mountain and missed the sights   We're taught to score a goal
Neither of us realized that the beginning is the top   Maybe just being is easier
Life is not to climb a mountain but to walk down   Maybe it will just happen
Certain perversions turn us upside down   Guidance not goals
Life is whatever we make it   Down not up
We all started at the top   Rest to find
Remember this   Peace

60 – My brain made it a big deal, not me

What did someone not share with me that I expected them to share with me?

What do I not share, or compartmentalize?

How is this a heavy ominous burden?

Can it be light and playful?

My brain is excellent at reassigning significance to things
Specks are large compared to my place in the universe
I was given the tool of language for it
Language is limited

61 – Money is a way to share

I have a billion dollars

Now what?

I have $100 to my name

Now what?

The perpetual irony of money is that I spend so much time thinking about it
Money is whatever my heart and soul want it to be, to be at peace with it
Money could be an option for warmth in the fireplace when it's obsolete
Money removed the human connection of bartering to us save time
Money is a temporary expansion of my external expressive aptitude
Chipotle removed the human connection further for more money
White or brown rice? Brown or Black beans? Genius or silence?
I'll know when I have a clear relationship with it
Money can be the root of ego if I'm unaware
Money isn't the root of anything
I am the root of every thing
Root myself in myself
I'm right and wrong
A headless chicken
Money is energy
Redefine money
To be free
Freedom

62 – Not trying can be petrifying

What happens if I do my worst?

What if I don't try?

Is that scary?

Boo!

63 – A misguided best can bring out the worst

When I don't do my job to the best of my abilities, am I stealing from my employer?

When did I do my best in something?

What do I do my best for?

How do I do my best?

Doing my brains best brings a fleeting satisfaction
But… best is an absolute
So then what?
Not trying?

64 – It has no motive

Life has been described through the ages by all different people with different lenses
Heartbreak, hard, begins at 40, going to kill you, a secret, perfect, a bitch, a process,
A tightrope, wild, crazy, a rollercoaster, a box of chocolates, fun, freedom
Vulnerable, precious, a gift, living, a journey, a path, a river, it just is, love
Life happening for me creates expectation
Life happening for me is delusional
Sell my expectations
Sell my delusions
Buy my soul
Buy myself

What motivates me to work?

"What do you do?" could be interpreted as "What are your problems in life? I want to share mine."

What's my freedom worth?

If my work is based on comparison, walk away but don't count the steps
If my work is based on efficiency, take the long way to walk away
If my work is based in both, run in a zig zag
Creativity is the future after automation

If I want my freedom   Give myself up
To create I support   Do not follow
To define I depend   Be guided

65 – Formalities are rigid, move yourself

I'm asking you, the reader, how are you right now?
This instant as you read this

How are you, right now?

Is there someone I see daily, but haven't asked how they are?

It doesn't know formality
It doesn't know motive

If I could describe life in one word, what would it be?
Life is…

66 – If I don't mean it, I smile quietly

What do I appreciate?

What's something someone did for me they didn't need to?

What was a beautiful accident?

What debt would be difficult for me to repay?

Recognizing is to identify something or someone previously seen
In most cases, appreciation has turned into simply identifying
Appreciating is truly to be grateful or thankful for
Appreciation is sometimes a buzzword, cliché
Stop the fake smiles
A fake smile is fear
Don't be afraid
Be original

67 – The Kool Aid is still laced with cyanide

Am I stressed at my job?

Sunday, Monday, Tuesday, Wednesday, Thursday, Friday, Saturday, Sunday, Monday, Tuesday, Wednesday, Thursday, Friday, Saturday, Sunday, Monday, Tuesday, Wednesday, Thursday, Friday, Saturday, Sunday, Monday, Tuesday, Wednesday, Thursday, Friday, Saturday, Sunday, Monday, Tuesday, Wednesday, Thursday, Friday, Saturday…
It's designed to be a loop and it made me one
Am I sure it's my stress and not theirs?
Where did I adopt it from?

Whose stress is it?

Stagnant emotionless machines pushing buttons and following up
Never truly know the person or make a real connection
Never talk religion or politics in business
Never bring emotion into business
Business as usual
Be unusual again
Let's get weird

68 – Intestines are a metaphor for life

What validates me?

Where could I grow up, or better yet be like a child, and go with my gut?

Where do I go against my gut because I'm too strong to let it guide me?

Growth of my brain is unsatisfying and I want more
Growth of my consciousness is curious and loving
My gut is my internal river always flowing
Swimming upstream could make me ill
Vulnerability is my boat to health
Strength is a slow track to illness
Openness brings me health
No motor necessary
Slow myself down
Get on and sail
There's the sun
My waves
Calming

I don't need validation from anyone
I get validation at the parking lot
Sex is not validation
I validate myself

69 – The natural choice is the hardest because we do not choose

I focus so much on the outcome I miss the process
What are my outcomes?

Do I remember being present and loving during sex and not racing to… finish?

If I could never have sex again the rest of my life, would I still be with them?

There are nine year old girls that want labiaplasties because of comparison
There are men making their penises limp and frail using vacuum pumps
It's not my shame or judgment, please deny it, deny their norms
If I mainly watch the envelopment during sex that's a warning
If eye contact during sex is uncomfortable that's a warning
If sex is only for physical sensation that's a warning
If sex is scheduled that's a warning
Sex has no goal or outcome
Sex is about union of souls
Break your sexual norms
Sex is infinite and finite
Sex is universal
Sex is natural
Sex is sacred
Sex is bond
Sex is fun
Have sex
Or don't

70 – Listening, watching, tasting, and feeling keep me from the smell of the roses

Do I remember when I stopped consciously doing everything?
What would that feel like?

When I'm like water a cup of water a cup of water can be more entertaining than a movie
Try too hard to balance and I end up controlling

What's something I'm juggling?

Some people juggle their way through life
The option to put the balls down exists

Can I put the balls down?

Can I stop bouncing the ball?

What is out of balance in my life?

What does being balanced look like to me?

Be like water and let everything be even, but not perfectly balanced
The terms introvert and extrovert are labels nothing more
Don't care too much about what doesn't matter
Too much significance is given to mountains
Too much significance is given to mole hills
Extroverts are good at creating diversions
Diverting attention to themselves
Introverts are good at hiding it
Hiding from some deep pain
The real me is balanced
No need to divert
No need to hide

72 – Walking as the crow flies is dangerous without wings

Who understands themselves?
Do I?
How?

It's not a straight path and different for everyone
Where am I most efficient?

A billion texts sent per week, how many of those texts are sent by me while driving?
I'm looking forward to the next red-light so I can focus on ruining my focus
The brain needs to know, control, prevent, and make efficient
Efficiency taken too far becomes neurosis and obsession
Efficiency taken too far becomes texting and driving
Efficiency taken too far can become texting and…
If it buzzes I must check it
Stop checking it
Drive yourself

73 – Be centered, not perfect

Am I afraid of being 'just' ok?

Am I ok?

What should be a certain way?

Not is the only absolute I should ever use, so is a triple negative a truth and not a positive?
Right and wrong are for them, it and responsibility are for you
External certainty and security are matters of the future
Wanting certainty and security breeds judgments
Wanting certainty and security breeds fears   Judgment vanishes when I accept what is
Never always feel good, a path to freedom   Being mediocre can feel like euphoria
Absolutes are limited unless negated   I was afraid of being ok
I am unlimited   Now I'm ok

74 – "How do you survive without a phone?!"

Do I compulsively look at my phone for directions to somewhere I've been?
Do I pull out my phone in new social situations?
Do I check it even when it doesn't buzz?

The more I need to know of the outside, the less I know of my inside
How do I get to know a person if they don't know themselves?
Vegetation is one of the keys to getting out of a vegetative state
WTF is he talking about? Eat more broccoli? Well yes, but...
Nature is a messy, and we're a mess without it to rebalance us
Watching TV sitting on a couch makes me a vegetable
How many of us walk and drive using our phones?
Vegetables walking and driving sounds dangerous
Be curious, take a breath, and be present with it
If I say I'm not watching TV, I'm in denial
Take a break from knowing and googling
"But I'm just checking something"
Check yourself

What do I know?

Where am I barely making it?

Needing to know about the future for security is not curiosity
Needing to know about the future to sound important sucks
Needing to know about the future for security is survival
Curiosity is the opposite of a need for security
There are no lions or tigers chasing me

75 – A new form of loneliness

I never judge anyone or myself on social media, right?

Who did I last judge?
Why?

Why questions about myself lead to endless delusion
What was the judgment really based in?
It's usually a mirror of my brain

What are my why questions?

Isn't it annoying when kids ask "why?" ten times just for attention? Or is it endearing?
Is asking myself why a subconscious cry for my own attention?
Could it be!?!

Write the names of EVERYONE I've ever been jealous of since my first memory
If I've never been jealous: a grudge is the same thing as jealousy, sorry, I have
My brain was jealous of something they had it wanted
I'm not actually jealous of them
My brain was
Real me
Free

76 – The modern antithesis of it

Do I take pictures to share inspiration, or do I take pictures to feel important and needed?

How much of my time on social media is spent truly connecting?

How long can I live without social media?

How many times a day do I compare myself to someone else?

Can you please move that spaghetti strand so I can get a lit picture of this savage dinner?
Thanks, now let's not talk to each other for the rest of the night and stare at our phones
But that's awkward and we feel people staring at us, so let's stare back and throw shade
Better yet, because they aren't using their phones like zombies lets think insecure goals
Still, let's not talk to each other, this is already so fleek and we don't know how to talk
Dating apps will make your thumb swole af and slay your communication skills
The universe doesn't care how many stamps are on my passport
The universe doesn't care how many bros I golf with
And it sure doesn't give a shit how many likes I get
I use my energy to converse and digest the food
Not get the perfect picture of it
Getting likes is rigged and fake
Perfection is fake

Judgment is something my heart wishes to eliminate in my identity that doesn't serve me
Judgment is something external my brain wants and doesn't have
Judgment is the brains fear of the unknown

The dictionary says judgment is sentencing another
We say judgment is self incarceration
It imprisons my heart
Free it

"I can't believe I had another drink, ate another piece, or spent an hour on my phone instead of…"
Really means "I want to change, but I don't know how because I've been taught not to talk to strangers. I won't talk with my future self because I don't know someone who doesn't drink, doesn't crave more food, or doesn't sit on their phone for hours when they would rather…"
Why can't I change this?
I can

"Look at her butt, wasting time and money on squats with her trainer. Her outfit is too revealing."
Really means "I'm not satisfied with my body and wish I had the time and money for a personal trainer or the discipline to have that because my body feels or looks unhealthy."
"Look at that ass in his gaudy luxury car"
Really means, "I want that"
Why can't I have that?
I can

"What's she doing?! She looks like she's crazy or on drugs. Let's get out of here."
Really means, "I wish I had the courage to do that, she's herself"
Why am I afraid?
I'm not

Why do I text and drive? I'm afraid of missing something? Can create anxiety

Why don't I go to the gym? I'm afraid of being seen? Can create depression

Why can't I follow my heart? My brain won't STFU? Can create discontent

Asking why can be an infinite loop
Judgment comes from asking why
Judgment comes from the brain
Wanting comes from the brain
It comes from the heart
The heart doesn't judge
The heart doesn't want
The heart is aware

78 – Right or wrong, anticipation leads to judgment

Kindergarten, 1st grade, 2nd grade, 3rd grade, 4th grade, 5th grade, 6th grade, 7th grade, 8th grade...
I've been groomed my entire life to be a test taker and to study to predict the future
I've learned to be prepared for every possible outcome and to see the future
What's next? What else could there be? What did I miss?.
Now is next, stop testing myself and others
Comparison is judgment
I can't know the future
Comparison is a test
Judgment is a test
Stop testing

I go to pick up food at the grocery store   I go to the gym to look better
I get in a car accident on the way   I drop the weights
People judge me   People judge me
Insurance   Pick them up

Her dress is what she likes... maybe I'm insecure with my sexuality or body
I eat bad food and watch trashy shows because I felt insecure earlier
I judge myself

His sunglasses are what he likes... maybe I wish I had the confidence to wear them
I buy things I never wear because I felt insecure
I judge myself

This isn't happiness

What is?

Our brains chase happiness, chasing something that disappears is tiring
Without awareness judgment leads to more judgment
Anxiety and depression are from the brains fear
The brains fear of losing what's been built
Built by media, judgments, parenting
Fear of learning about myself
Fear of knowing myself
Judgment of myself
Fear of the future
Judgment of that
Fear of the past
Not of now

79 – My true center is simple

What's my truth?

How do I know it's true?

What feels simple to me?

The top salespeople try to help me feel like I'm enough, which insinuates I'm not… irony
I need complexity, I need more, I need a system to truly be enough… lol
Like race, intelligence is meant to make me feel like I'm not enough
Intelligence is simply the ability to get and use knowledge and skills
Anyone can get knowledge and skills because of… internet
Be wary of anything that hints that I'm not enough
Unguided brain pulls me from the center of me
External knowledge will eventually be obsolete
I know the things I need to know
Internal knowledge is freedom
I am simple at my center
Knowledge is complex
The brain is complex
Wisdom is simple

The word ego was introduced in 1714
It's become a holier than thou word
"Oh, that's just her ego talking"
Although, male egos talk more
It's just a label for my brain
What if I didn't have one?
Who would I be?
Brainless?

80 – Stop for satisfaction, keep searching for discontent

Am I ok with silence?

Am I ok with silence without my phone, or anything to do?

Am I ok with nothingness?

What do I think I'm seeking or looking for?

Happiness comes and goes, that's being human
Unless you're medicated or hypnotized
That's called delusional happiness
I cannot medicate my way to it
I cannot affirm my way to it
I cannot mantra myself to it
I cannot sing my way to it
Happiness is not it
Happiness will go
Let's learn to stay
With myself

81 - My love is not a language, language is limited, and love is unlimited

Social media, games, compulsive phone checking
Overloading my senses will hide me from myself
Nothing my brain feels from my senses will last
Eating the trashy food I know is bad
To feel that numbing feeling again
The pleasure will end quickly
The pain can remain
Judgment is pain
Overload
Physical
Disease
Mental
Illness

Seeing the stunning man or woman disappear in my rearview mirror
Feeling my new clothes age and fall apart after too many washings
Smelling my favorite meal and then nothing when it's done
Hearing them play live and then the silence after
Tasting my favorite food and then it's gone
These things disappear into my memory
Memories are thoughts in my brain
Let go of definitions of memories
Definitions that confine
Memories of the past

Information tried to overload me daily and I refuse it
In order to find it, I've got to calm the brain
It doesn't disappear in my rearview mirror
It doesn't fall apart or need to be washed
It's that warming feeling, its tears of joy
It never stops and isn't finished
It's the voice found in silence
Take the power back
Be curious about me
Bewilder myself
Don't Google it
Imagine that
Imagination
I'll find it
I'll stop